The Best Work-From-Home Jobs For 2020

The Best Work-From-Home Jobs For 2020

144 Legitimate Remote Jobs That
Are (Almost) Always Hiring

Annie Sandmeier

Copyright © 2019 by Annie Sandmeier

All rights reserved. This book or any portion thereof may not be reproduced or used in any manner whatsoever without the express written permission of the publisher except for the use of brief quotations in a book review.

Although the author and publisher have made every effort to ensure that the information in this book was correct at press time, the author and publisher do not assume and hereby disclaim any liability to any party for any loss, damage, or disruption caused by errors or omissions, whether such errors or omissions result from negligence, accident, or any other cause.

Please note: As of this publication, all links should lead directly to the job site. The author is not responsible for moved or broken links that may occur after publication. All job descriptions come directly from the company's job listing(s).

Editing by Ashley Romereim

Contents

Foreword ix
How to Use This Book xiii
Customer Service Intro 1
    Customer Service Jobs 3
Teaching & Education Intro 11
    Teaching & Education Jobs 13
Flexible & On-Demand Work Intro 19
    Flexible & On-Demand Jobs 21
Bookkeeping & Virtual Assistance Intro 25
    Bookkeeping & Virtual Assistance Jobs 27
Sales Intro 31
    Sales Jobs 33
Transcription Intro 41
    Transcription Jobs 43
Writing Intro 49
    Writing Jobs 51
Why I Advise Against MLMs 57
About Annie 61
About Side Hustle Mom 63
References 65

To Brandon: Thank you for always supporting me and my random, sometimes wacky ideas and dreams (a la Side Hustle Mom). I love you.

To Jackson, Gabe, and our angel baby, Michael James: You are the reason for everything I do. Thanks for letting me be your mama and for inspiring me daily.

Foreword

Ever since I can remember, I have wanted to be a mom.

Come to find out, motherhood isn't a traditional college degree, so when it came time to graduate high school and move onto the next big thing, I opted for a degree in communications (namely broadcast journalism). While I absolutely loved my college classes and working at the campus TV station, I later discovered the world of broadcast news was NOT for me (a la interning in Denver the summer of the Aurora theater shooting) so I wasn't completely devastated when I was 23, newly married, and discovered we had a baby on the way.

At the time, I was working at our small-town TV station but was laid off when I was six months pregnant, which is when I began working part-time at a Catholic radio station. Between my husband's full-time job (which did have excellent benefits, Praise the Lord) and my working 20 hours a week, we were living below the poverty line so I knew I would have to continue working even after our baby arrived, shattering any dreams I had of being a full-time stay-at-home mom. Despite not being able to stay home full-time, my husband and I figured out a split schedule, so one of us was always home with the baby, which calmed my nerves as our due date approached.

We welcomed Baby Jackson in December 2013, exactly two weeks early and three days before Christmas.

ANNIE SANDMEIER

One week later, my husband interviewed for a job in Denver as a network engineer, which had a starting pay of more than twice what he was making at the time.

One week after that, he was offered and accepted the position, meaning we would be moving states with our soon-to-be one-month-old in tow.

Reliving these days (which were paired with an undiagnosed case of postpartum depression) makes me tired.

While my husband had a great job with good pay, we were now renting in one of the most expensive cities in the country, so I knew I still needed to do something to help with our finances so we could one day afford to buy a home.

That was when I took the reins and figured out ways to work from home around my son's schedule.

I started by working as a publicist/marketer/web designer for my hometown museum.

Later I began writing for a start-up website that is now one of the most popular travel sites on the web. (As of this writing, I have been with them for 4 1/2 years and am getting ready to take an all-expenses-paid company trip to Nashville... working from home isn't too bad!)

I worked as a copywriter and managing editor for a friend's tech blog.

About 3 1/2 years into my work-from-home journey, I started Side Hustle Mom, which opened my eyes even more to the world of remote work and its endless possibilities. Before beginning Side Hustle Mom, I had a general idea of what work-from-home jobs were available, but I NEVER thought the opportunities are as endless as they are!

In my 2+ years of research and sourcing, I have discovered hundreds of different opportunities, varying from marketing and writing to customer service and sales. While all of these jobs are relatively easy to Google, I wanted to do my fellow mamas (plus dads, students, retirees, and those just wanting to work in their pajamas!) a favor by rounding them all up in one place, which is when I decided to write this book - a collection of 144 companies who are almost always hiring and offer legitimate work-from-home positions. (In the two years that I have done Side Hustle Mom, I have clocked several hundred hours researching and writing, so if I can use those sleepless nights to save someone else time and energy, it was all worth it!)

Being a stay-at-home mom is by far the most gratifying thing I have/will ever do. I am the first person my boys see when they wake up and the last person they see before they fall asleep. I volunteer in my son's kindergarten class every week and attend our church's mom's group every Thursday morning. The boys and I host and attend more play dates than I can count. Almost every day, we do something impromptu, whether it be going to the library, playing at the Denver Children's Museum, or simply baking a batch of cookies for lunch.

Nothing in this world makes me happier than being my husband's wife and boys' mom, and I want EVERY mom who wants to do the same thing to be able to do it!

You CAN have it all: the family, the job, the [insert your biggest dreams and goals here] -- and I hope that this book can help or inspire you to do it.

Happy hunting, Side Hustle Mom (dads, students, and YOU!) -- you've got this!

Annie

How to Use This Book

You're busy, and I get it, which is why I want to make this book as short, sweet, and straightforward as possible.

This book is a list of 144 of some of the best and most legitimate work-from-home jobs and companies out there. Since openings can change daily (or even hourly!), I sought out to find some of the most well-respected companies and businesses that almost always have positions open, such as SyncScript, Philips, and TaxJar.

If you bought this as an ebook, your life just got a whole lot easier, as each company name is hyperlinked, meaning you can simply click the title and be re-directed to their job site. Easy peasy lemon squeezy, right?

If you love the physical feel of a book (as do I) and bought a hard copy, you have one extra step, as you will have to manually type the URL (found at the bottom of each listing) on your phone, computer, or laptop. I know, I know, I'm sorry... At least your book smells a lot nicer than a tablet, right?

This book is broken up into different book categories, including:

    Customer Service
    Teaching & Education
    Flexible & On-Demand Work

ANNIE SANDMEIER

    Bookkeeping & Virtual Assistance
    Sales
    Transcription
    Writing

While you may be leaning toward one category over another, I highly encourage you to browse all the listings, read the descriptions, and -- if it seems like a great fit -- send in your resumé.

Should I quit blabbing so you can start applying?

Done.

CUSTOMER SERVICE INTRO

Do you consider yourself a people person?

Are you a problem solver who thrives on fixing things?

Maybe you just have a calm demeanor and a pleasant voice?

If any of the above sounds like you, a work-from-home customer service position may be the perfect job for you!

With tens of thousands of companies around the world needing assistance with customer service and satisfaction, returns, and general inquiries, there is always a need for customer service representatives, making it a generally easy (and profitable) field to join.

What does it take to work in customer service? Typically, all you need is a high-speed internet connection, a headset, Monday through Friday availability (usually), and you are on your way to a successful customer service career!

Please note: As of this publication, all links should lead directly to the job site. The author is not responsible for moved or broken links that may occur after publication. All job descriptions come directly from the company's job listing(s).

Customer Service Jobs

1. <u>15Five: Customer Support Specialist:</u> 15Five is seeking a passionate Customer Support Representative to help support the next generation of continuous performance management and employee engagement software for 15Five customers. The primary focus of the role is to serve as a trusted advocate to our customers by handling technical issues and educating end users.

    https://jobs.lever.co/15five

2. <u>Aha!: Various Positions:</u> As a member of the Aha! team, you will jump into a breakthrough and profitable software company. We are changing the way the world's best-known companies build and market products customers love. It has been an amazing journey and we have been humbled by our rapid growth. Apply for one of the roles below if you want to join us on this adventure.

    https://www.aha.io/company/careers/current-openings

3. <u>Alorica: Customer Service Representative:</u> Passion. Performance. Possibilities. In your PJs. As an Alorica Work-at-Home team member, you get the flexibility to balance work and life while having access to all the tools and resources you need to deliver insanely great customer experiences. While we offer plenty of opportunities for Work-at-Home customer service careers, many of our corporate roles can be conducted virtually from home as well.

    https://www.alorica.com/careers/work-at-home/

4. <u>Amazon: Customer Service Associate:</u> An Amazon Customer Service Associate is a critical part of our mission to deliver timely, accurate and professional customer service to all Amazon customers. This vital position requires an action-oriented, flexible problem-solver who will assist customers in expediting orders and correcting post-sales problems. Associates communicate with customers primarily through phone and email and utilize a variety of software tools to navigate customer accounts, research and review policies and communicate effective solutions in a fun and fast-paced environment.

    https://www.amazon.jobs/en/locations/virtual-locations?

5. <u>American Express: Virtual Travel Consultant/Customer Service:</u> If you have a flair for exceptional customer service and an aptitude for learning and natural curiosity, this role is for you. With an intensive 11-week paid training and mentoring program, here's your chance to become a highly-skilled Travel Consultant. Are you up for the challenge to join a leader in the travel industry?

    https://jobs.americanexpress.com/virtual?

6. <u>Arise: Various:</u> Arise Virtual Solutions provides a technology platform that connects customer service representatives running small call center businesses with prestigious clients, many of which are Fortune 500 companies.

https://www.ariseworkfromhome.com/customer-service-opportunities/

7. <u>Automattic: Client Service:</u> Transforming publishing on the web is no small task. Our goal is to build relationships based on trust, which result in happy, passionate, loyal customers and colleagues. We do this through listening to their needs and guiding them to the fullest use of the products we offer. We are looking for people with

the right mix of compassion, writing skills, and technical knowledge to get the job done.

https://automattic.com/work-with-us/

8. BCD Travel: Corporate Travel Consultant & Various: The Corporate Travel Consultant is responsible for accurately and efficiently handling incoming requests via multiple channels (some phone, mostly email). The travel consultant is the primary point of contact for the customer and provides active travel consultation towards the business customers, including providing travel details and up-selling of related product. This position demonstrates a strong understanding and applicability of all areas of responsibility. Works independently on requests. Provides assistance to team members as requested.

https://recruiting.adp.com/srccar/public/RTI.home?

9. Bizzabo: Customer Support Representative: Can you handle managing multiple projects, no problem? We are looking for a Customer Support Representative to join the Bizzabo.

https://www.bizzabo.com/careers#iframeposition

10. Ciox Health: Audit Specialist: The Auditing Specialist will respond to consulting and education needs related to coding quality, compliance assessments, external payer reviews, coding education, interim coding management, and coding workflow operations reviews. Offer meaningful information to meet customer expectations, including identifying and proposing solutions for customer issues. Develop and maintain account relationships through responsiveness and calm, reflective work practices. Work cooperatively with the Data Quality & Coding Compliance leadership and scheduling for optimal services outcome.

https://careers-cioxhealth.icims.com/jobs/search?

11. <u>Concentrix: Sales & Service Representative:</u> We have three types of work at home positions that we hire for regularly: Sales & Service, Customer Service and Technical Support Representatives. Every position we have is centered around providing excellent customer service and some positions are more sales or technically focused. Your answers to the questions during the application process, your qualifications, and your experience will all be reviewed as part of the evaluation process to determine which one is the best fit for you.

    https://careers.concentrix.com/work-at-home

12. <u>Conduent: Customer Service Representative:</u> As a member of the corporate team, you'll focus on enhancing the relationship with our clients as we provide outstanding business solution services.

    https://jobs.conduent.com/search-jobs/remote?

13. <u>Cruise.com: Customer Service Agent:</u> This position requires at least 1 year of recent cruise industry or call center experience either in sales or customer service. Please note related cruise industry experience is required. Our Customer Service Agents answer incoming calls from customers and happily help resolve problems, provide information, and answer questions. Our team members take pride in assisting our valued customers while providing a high level of service, patience, professionalism, and kindness.

    https://www.cruise.com/cruise-information/employment/

14. <u>Dell: Various:</u> Technology now makes it possible to work from almost anywhere and Dell's Connected Workplace program allows eligible team members to do just that, by choosing the work style that best fulfills their needs on the job and in their personal lives.

    https://jobs.dell.com/category/remote-jobs

THE BEST WORK-FROM-HOME JOBS FOR 2020

15. Fisico: Virtual Customer Care Specialist: If you're looking for a flexible, work-from-home position that improves peoples' lives… then this will be the most exciting post you read today. Here's why…

    https://fisicoinc.com/virtual-customer-care-specialist

16. Frontline Education: Client Support Specialist: Reporting to a Support Manager, the Client Support Specialist is responsible for customer inquiries, identifying and troubleshooting problems, and providing advice to assist users of Frontline Education systems.

    https://careers-frontlinetechnologies.icims.com/jobs/search?

17. HSN.com: Customer Care: This team is the heartbeat of our company. They provide best-in-class customer service 24/7. Their in-depth knowledge of our products and policies create lasting relationships with our customers.

    https://jobs.hsn.com/category/customer-and-business-services-jobs

18. HVMN: Customer Success Associate: HVMN is hiring a part-time (~20 hours per week), remote-option Customer Success Associate, reporting to our Head of Customer Success. As a Customer Success Associate, you are the voice of HVMN and have a direct relationship with our customers.

    https://jobs.lever.co/hvmn

19. Liveops: Agent: Join a national team of agents delivering customer service, support and sales—all from the comfort of your home office.

    https://join.liveops.com/work-from-home-call-center-jobs/

20. LiveSurface: Support - Billing and Sales: LiveSurface is an industry leader in visualization and image creation tools for creatives. We

blend leading technology with hand-curated content to provide real-time photorealistic visualization to our users. At our heart, we are a team of creatives that thrive on transforming challenging problems into beautifully implemented solutions.

    https://www.livesurface.com/jobs.php?k=support.billing

21. NexRep: Virtual Contact Center Agent: We have great opportunities in customer service and sales and are looking for just the right match for our mutual third-party clients. Our clients range from products and services in branded retail, consumer electronics, direct response, catalog and direct mail, e-commerce, travel and hospitality. You can be an agent providing customer service or sales from the comfort of your own home. Please join us at NexRep, the most reputable and fastest growing work-at-home contact center in America!

    https://nexrep.com/become-a-contact-center-agent/

22. Quartzy: Customer Support Specialist: Quartzy is seeking a Customer Support Specialist to ensure that our customers are getting the best level of service possible. We are experiencing tremendous growth, and in this role, you'll have the chance to help us define our fulfillment processes as our company scales.

    https://www.quartzy.com/careers

23. Sutherland: Various: Sutherland remote jobs include: Licensed Insurance Agent, Customer Service, and more.

    https://www.sutherlandglobal.com/about-us/remote-engagement-for-job-seekers

24. The Hartford: Various Positions: You're a driven and motivated problem solver ready to pursue meaningful work. You strive to make

an impact every day – not only at work, but in your personal life and community too. If this sounds like you, then you've landed in the right place.

https://thehartford.taleo.net/careersection/2/jobsearch.ftl

25. <u>Transcom: Customer Service Representative:</u> You'll be the friendly voice of our Telecommunications client to support their customers with smartphones, tablets, and computers. As a CSR, you'll listen to the caller and use your technical expertise as well as passion for outstanding customer service to answer questions about products and services, or troubleshoot technical issues to find solutions.

https://www.transcom.com/en/careers

26. <u>U-Haul: Roadside Assistance Agent:</u> As the leaders of the do-it-yourself moving industry, U-Haul Roadside Assistance works hard to ensure our customer's safety and experience is handled with professionalism, care and support. At times, unexpected hurdles arise that warrant our Roadside Assistance team to step in and guide our customer back en route to their destination. U-Haul Roadside Assistance team members handle back-to-back incoming calls and initiate outbound calls to customers and roadside assistance service providers. As we actively listen to the customer's experience, it is vital that clear detailed notes are built on every call for proper documentation purposes.

https://jobs.uhaul.com/OpenJobs

27. <u>Vivint Smart Home: Customer Solutions Technical Support:</u> Note: Must live in a 100 mile radius of Lindon, UT and work a minimum of 30 hours a week.

https://vivint.wd5.myworkdayjobs.com/vivintjobs

28. <u>Working Solutions: Customer Care Agent:</u> For customers, the experience is everything. With our on-demand contact center solutions, excellent sales and service elevate your business. Rise above the competition.

    https://jobs.workingsolutions.com

29. <u>Xerox: Customer Care:</u> We're actively seeking high-quality individuals for work at home opportunities.

    https://www.xerox.com/en-us/jobs/work-from-home

TEACHING & EDUCATION INTRO

Did you know that it is possible to teach outside of your traditional classroom? Thanks to adjunct professors (a la online college courses), online public school, and the increasingly popular ESL courses, there has never been a better time to teach from home!

Do you have zero experience teaching but at least have your bachelor's degree in any major? Believe it or not, you are a perfect candidate for teaching online, as most of these schools do not require teaching experience but rather any degree, high-speed internet, and a fun and engaging personality.

Please note: As of this publication, all links should lead directly to the job site. The author is not responsible for moved or broken links that may occur after publication. All job descriptions come directly from the company's job listing(s).

Teaching & Education Jobs

1. A Pass Education: K-12 Science, Social Studies, Math, or ELA Associate: Qualifications are: a degree related to the subject area, K-12 teaching experience, item writing experience, and availability to write and respond to editorial requests about 2-5 hours per day. Ideal candidates will have knowledge of DOK levels, Common Core, and/or NGSS.

    https://apasseducation.com/job-openings/

2. Adtalem Global Education: Higher Education: The purpose of Adtalem Global Education is to empower students to achieve their goals, find success, and make inspiring contributions to our global community.

    https://www.adtalem.com/careers.html

3. Aim 4 A: Tutor (Various): Aim Academics is looking for part-time and full-time tutors to provide in center tutoring at one of our locations and online tutoring services to students worldwide. If you have a mastery of ANY subject, we would like to hear from you!

    http://www.aim4a.com/tutors.php

4. Avantpage: Translator: We are continually looking for translators with the right blend of skills, experience and commitment to contribute to our mission of delivering the highest quality translation services in the industry. If you are a qualified translator looking for

an exciting career and opportunity to work with us, we'd love to hear from you.

https://www.avantpage.com/about/careers/

5. Cambly: English Tutor: Cambly gives you instant access to native English speakers over video chat, so you can learn and gain confidence!

https://www.cambly.com/en/tutors?lang=en

6. Class100: English Tutor: CLASS100 expertly partners with public schools across China to deliver technology into their English classes.

https://en.class100.com/

7. DaDa: English Tutor: Founded in 2013, DaDa is the leading online English education platform based in China. Since its inception, DaDa's mission is to be the best online international school in China through one-on-one student-teacher pairing, world-class teaching content, and industry-leading two-way interactive learning platform. DaDa is the proud partner of Pearson Education, McGraw-Hill Education, Oxford University Press, National Geographic Learning, Highlights, and many other prestigious publishers and learning centers.

https://www.dadaabc.com/teacher/landing

8. Eagle Productivity Solutions: Curriculum/ Content Leads (Instructional Design): The team at Eagle works to design and deliver industry-leading training content, from live, instructor-led training to video to dynamic reference pieces. As a Lead, you will be responsible for helping a team of writers successfully execute a curriculum development project.

https://eagleproductivity.com/careers.html

THE BEST WORK-FROM-HOME JOBS FOR 2020

9. <u>Earlybirds: Various:</u> Besides cooperation with our academic partners, Earlybirds offers international standard programs to individual student. We have both English and drama courses every term, professional theatre shows and summer school every year.

    http://www.earlybirds.cn/careers.html

10. <u>EducationFirst: English Tutor:</u> If you join us, you will need to provide documentation of your Bachelor's degree and a 40 hour TEFL certificate (or higher). We're happy to answer any questions you have about finishing a TEFL certification!

    https://ef.secure.force.com/onlineteacher2?c=

11. <u>eNotes: Educator and Academic Writer:</u> Our Educators are real teachers, scholars, and professional writers who share their knowledge with students all over the world. Join our team and use your academic expertise to help thousands of struggling students while earning money (pay ranges from $5–$37 per answer). As an Educator, you get to decide how much you work and what type of questions you want to tackle.

    https://www.enotes.com/jax/index.php/users/register?eventHandler=educatorapply

12. <u>gogokid: English Tutor:</u> We offer one-on-one online language lessons based on the U.S. Common Core State Standards and the Chinese standard curriculum through a virtual classroom infused with cutting-edge AI technology.

    https://teacher.gogokid.com/

13. <u>Golden Voice English: English Tutor:</u> As a GVE English Tutor, you will provide exceptional online English lessons to Chinese children via a video conferencing tool. You will be able to deliver unique,

engaging, and innovative e-Learning lessons using GVE-provided teaching materials, resources, and techniques. This is a part-time, independent contractor role, working between the hours of 6:00 am to 10:00am (EST) on Monday-Saturday.

https://gveoe.com/gvenew/

14. <u>Great Minds: Various:</u> At Great Minds, we believe that every child is capable of greatness. When you join the team, you will be part of a rapidly growing, mission-driven organization. This mission to improve education for America's schoolchildren is what inspires us each day.

https://greatminds.recruitee.com/#/

15. <u>iTutorGroup: English Tutor:</u> Connecting teachers from across the globe to students in Asia. Join the fast-growing world of online education with iTutorGroup.

https://join.itutorgroup.com/#/?fromwhere=groupsite

16. <u>Lime English: English Tutor:</u> This job role involves teaching English online to students in China, ranging in age from 5-15 years old.

https://twosigmas.com/g-job/
lime-english-teaching-english-online/okeechobee-florida/

17. <u>Noom, Inc.: Virtual Health Coach:</u> We have created a unique and constantly evolving wellness product, so expect to be constantly challenged! Our team of Health Coaches are heavily involved in rapid prototyping and experimenting with new, cutting-edge coaching tactics and methodologies. Expect to work in a fast-paced environment with constant new projects to tackle. Expect to hear from thousands of people whose lives you changed. You are the face of Noom and sit at the intersection between technology, behavior

change, and our users. You'll work closely with our users every step of their journey, helping them identify goals that will allow them to achieve their ultimate health goals.

https://www.noom.com/careers/job/

18. QKids: English Tutor: QKids connects 600,000+ Chinese young learners between 4 - 12 years old with you and thousands of other online teachers, tutors, educators, stay at home parents, college students, and all those who have a passion for teaching. If you like starting your day with smiling faces of curious kids, join the QKids family today!

https://teacher.qkids.net/job

19. Rosetta Stone: Language Tutor (Various): With a work environment that encourages and nurtures creativity, great ideas take flight and become products and services built from the bottom up. Working for Rosetta Stone means that your opportunities are limitless.

https://rosettastone.wd5.myworkdayjobs.com/Rosetta_Stone

20. Skooli: Math Tutor: Tutoring on Skooli is easy. Students can schedule sessions in advance or request instant help if you're online. Tutor students one-on-one from anywhere with an internet connection using your computer.

https://www.skooli.com/for_tutors

21. Star Teachers: Various: Star Teachers, Inc. is a U.S. based recruiting and teaching resources management company. We hire American and Canadian English teachers who teach international students online as well as in classrooms in China.

https://starteachersinc.recruitee.com/

22. <u>Tutree: Math Tutor:</u> Tutree provides an app that allows students or parents to find and schedule a local, qualified peer tutor--at the tap of a button.

    http://www.tutree.com/tutoring-jobs/#popup1

23. <u>VIPKid: English Tutor:</u> Teach English to children in China, online, on your schedule, and all from home.

    https://www.vipkid.com/teach

24. <u>Voxy: English Teacher:</u> The Voxy live instruction team delivers best-in-class ESL instruction to groups and individual learners. We believe in individualized instruction delivered through authentic content, not a one-size-fits-all approach. Our learners include students and professionals that span five continents.

    https://boards.greenhouse.io/voxy

25. <u>Yup: Homework Tutor:</u> Yup is revolutionizing education by providing all students instant affordable mobile access to personalized learning. We help students get to the "aha" moment, not just an answer. Join our team and make an impact.

    https://www.yup.com/become-tutor

FLEXIBLE & ON-DEMAND WORK INTRO

Are you short on time and looking for something to supplement your income here and there?

Maybe the holiday season is fast approaching (as it seems to do every year), and you would prefer to pay for everything with cash?

Have you been promising the kids a trip to Disney and need to start saving?

In this day and age, such a thing as on-demand work exists, meaning you can work on a contract basis and on your own schedule (think DoorDash, Uber, etc.) and choose the kind of jobs YOU want to do! From delivering flowers for companies to stocking shelves at the store, you are sure to find your perfect part-time gig on the following pages.

Please note: As of this publication, all links should lead directly to the job site. The author is not responsible for moved or broken links that may occur after publication. All job descriptions come directly from the company's job listing(s).

Flexible & On-Demand Jobs

1. <u>Acorn:</u> Acorn was founded by a working dad, but it's for everyone who needs flexibility in their schedule. Workers who double as caregivers for elderly parents. Moms who've been out of the workforce and are ready to come back. People who long to work in Silicon Valley but live in Kansas City. Baby boomers who would enjoy the perks of retirement but thrive on the sense of purpose they get from working. Young people who desire to live abroad while still advancing their nascent careers. Runners aiming to train for marathons. Creative writers penning the next great American novel. Pretty much everyone who is career-driven and wants more control over their time and their lives. Whether they work remote, reduced hours, or on a flexible schedule, Acorn members are not contract workers. They become full-fledged employees of their new company. This allows them to continue to grow in their career, while still living their best lives.

    https://acornwork.typeform.com

2. <u>Amazon Flex:</u> Deliver with Amazon. Be your own boss. Great earnings. Flexible hours. Make more time for whatever drives you.

    https://flex.amazon.com/

3. Fancy Hands: Fancy Hands is a team of US-based assistants at your fingertips. Use any device, at any time of day, and our assistants will tackle anything on your to-do list!

   https://www.fancyhands.com/

4. Favor (Texas): Favor is Texas' best delivery service with 50,000+ Runners in 100+ cities. Runners are more than delivery drivers -- we're hometown heroes with the power to make someone's day.

   https://favordelivery.com/

5. Gigsmart: GigSmart has two core missions. First of all, GigSmart wants to create a seamless, efficient, friendly employer/independent contractor marketplace that optimally matches employers seeking on-demand labor and individuals willing to provide it. Secondly, GigSmart wants to develop an efficient system for charitable organizations to manage their volunteer needs while providing interested volunteers the ability to make themselves available.

   https://gigsmart.com/workers/

6. Graphite: Graphite is a platform that connects you with highly vetted independent consultants for on-demand work. Leading companies leverage our platform to access hard-to-find skills and expertise, add horsepower to their teams, and accelerate business performance.

   https://www.graphite.com/professional/signup

7. HelloTech: Earn money solving tech problems. A fun and flexible way to earn money on your own time!

   https://us.hellotech.com/techs

8. Jyve: Jyve is a Skills-as-a-Service platform that matches enterprise businesses' in-store execution needs with the right skilled labor at

THE BEST WORK-FROM-HOME JOBS FOR 2020

the right time. Operational in most of America, Jyve offers brands, retailers, and grocers fast access to certified skilled Jyvers who are trained to handle tasks ranging from merchandising to auditing to e-commerce order fulfillment.

https://jyve.com/become-a-jyver

9. <u>On Demand Staffing:</u> From the Indianapolis Motor Speedway and Lucas Oil Stadium in Indianapolis to Adesa Auto Auction in Tampa and Manheim Auto Auctions in San Antonio and Dallas, On Demand Staffing supplies over 30,000 people with jobs totaling half a million hours of work every month.

https://ondemandstaffing.jobs/

10. <u>Roadie:</u> We're the first nationwide delivery service that's "on-the-way" – making us faster, more flexible, and more scalable than traditional carriers and "on-demand" couriers. Our drivers have delivered to 11,000+ cities and towns nationwide – a larger footprint than Amazon Prime Now.

https://drive.roadie.com/signup

11. <u>Snagajob:</u> Thousands of companies are hiring right now. Start your job search today!

https://www.snagajob.com/

12. <u>So Many Errands:</u> So Many Errands is an online marketplace where you can hire errand runners to run errands for you OR you can become an errand runner and start making money!

https://www.somanyerrands.com/

13. Spare5: Earn money in your spare time with our free web and mobile apps.

    https://app.spare5.com/fives

14. Steady: Founded in the summer of 2017 by Adam Roseman, Michael Loeb, and Eric Aroesty, Steady is a new app for workers looking to supplement their income by taking part-time, one-time, anytime, and temporary jobs. The Steady app makes it easier for these workers to find the best work opportunities to build their careers, as well as manage and better understand their income.

    https://steadyapp.com/

15. Takl: Make money on your own schedule with Takl. Use your skills to help others complete small jobs and household chores.

    https://www.takl.com/

16. TaskRabbit: Be someone's hero today. Earn money by helping people with their everyday to-dos.

    https://www.taskrabbit.com/become-a-tasker

17. Wonolo: Don't let job schedules run your life. Wonolo connects you with immediate hourly or same day jobs from the biggest and best brands, allowing you to work where you want, when you want, for whomever you want.

    https://www.wonolo.com/find-work/

BOOKKEEPING & VIRTUAL ASSISTANCE INTRO

Be honest: How Type A are you? While I wish I possessed this organized, go-getting trait, I do not (where are my other Type B-ers at?!) and would turn to someone else to do my bookkeeping, scheduling, and organizing of my business and life.

Does this sound like something you could do?

Bookkeeping and virtual assisting jobs are the perfect fit for not only super organized individuals but also those with a background in accounting, marketing, and other clerical work.

Please note: As of this publication, all links should lead directly to the job site. The author is not responsible for moved or broken links that may occur after publication. All job descriptions come directly from the company's job listing(s).

Bookkeeping & Virtual Assistance Jobs

1. Belay Solutions: Virtual Assistant: BELAY was founded on this simple idea: there aren't just two options for work. We believe there's another way – what we call The Third Option. This option allows you to work from home (so you have far more opportunities to get work you love) while choosing how much you work. Whether you're a Virtual Assistant, Bookkeeper, or Web Specialist, we have clients right now who need the expertise and insight you bring to the table. And because you're remote, you can bring your knowledge from the kitchen table.

    https://realwaystoearnmoneyonline.com/virtual-assistant-jobs/

2. Boldly: Executive Assistant: Boldly's team of talented professionals has left behind the daily commute for the advantages of working remotely, and the flexibility that it allows them. As a world-class executive assistant, you'll support entrepreneurs, small business owners, and executives from successful companies with a wide range of tasks, and have the opportunity to develop new skill sets as you get exposure to a variety of companies and industries.

    https://boldly.com/milso-jobs/executive-assistant/

3. Dental Claimsupport: Remote Dental Billing: Dental ClaimSupport is seeking a self-motivated, detail-oriented Medical/Dental Billing Specialist who can positively impact our fast-growing dental billing company. The ideal candidate has at least 1 year of experience in the

dental/medical field, works well with others, understands insurance plans, and has a basic knowledge of insurance coding.

https://dentalclaimsupport.com/careers/remote

4. <u>Equivity: Administrative, Marketing, and Paralegal Virtual Assistants:</u> Equivity is on the lookout for virtual assistants that are resourceful, detail-oriented, proactive, and extremely organized. Equivity is a team of individuals dedicated to improving the lives of our clients so that they can focus on their priorities. Our virtual assistants take initiative and develop creative solutions that help our clients achieve these goals.

https://www.equivityva.com/about/careers/

5. <u>Konsus: Various:</u> Konsus is the world's first online workplace that puts the freelancers first. Unlike freelancer marketplace models, we work only with professional pre-qualified freelancers, who get access to a constant stream of incoming projects to choose from.

https://www.konsus.com/career

6. <u>Perssist: Assistant:</u> We are looking for smart people passionate about helping others with a great attitude and the ability to figure things out on your own.

https://www.perssist.com/jobs

7. <u>Supporting Strategies: Accounting Services:</u> Supporting Strategies currently has over 70 offices throughout the U.S. and is continuing to grow rapidly! This momentum has created exceptional opportunities for accountants who enjoy managing remote teams and working closely with a variety of clients. Consider joining us for a rewarding accounting career that offers interesting professional challenges with

optimal work-life balance. As our network of franchises grow, new team managers are integral to our continued success.

https://careers-supportingstrategies.icims.com/jobs/search?

8. TaxJar: Various Remote Roles: TaxJar is the leading technology solution for busy eCommerce sellers to manage sales tax and is trusted by more than 15,000 businesses. We were founded to help eCommerce owners spend less time on sales tax and more time growing the businesses they love. We're passionate about creating simple solutions and leveraging technology to solve complicated sales tax issues. We're not just about sales tax though, we're a technology-driven company focused on providing a great experience for both merchants and developers.We offer TaxJar Reports, a simple web-based reporting tool that organizes sales tax data into return-ready reports by state; AutoFile, a service that automatically files sales tax returns; and SmartCalcs API, a modern, accurate, sales tax API for developers to outsource sales tax rates and calculations. For developers, we have created a helpful API demo environment and also are fanatics about creating and maintaining great API documentation.

https://taxjar.workable.com/

9. Time Etc.: Virtual Assistant: If you have a background as a personal assistant, executive assistant, secretary, administrative assistant, or you have your own Virtual Assistant business, we want to hear from you.

https://timeetc.com/us/be-a-virtual-assistant/

10. Vasumo: Virtual Assistant: Working side-by-side we create meaningful connections with each other and our clients. We treat each other with consideration and respect, and we celebrate our differences.

We aim for excellence, and our love for what we do compels us to reach a higher standard. You can be proud of the work you do here.

https://vasumo.com/careers/

11. <u>Zirtual: Virtual Executive Assistant:</u> The Virtual Assistant is a vital member of Zirtual. The VA is the main point of contact with the client(s) and will work independently with the client(s). The VA will receive support from their assigned Account Supervisor, who will assist the VA/client relationship with plan modifications, questions, and provide feedback on quality, delegation issues, and more.

https://www.zirtual.com/jobs

SALES INTRO

Arguably the most profitable of work-from-home jobs is sales, where you can earn not only a base pay but commissions as well. No experience in sales? This typically is not a problem, as many companies prefer someone new who can be trained by their particular company!

Please note: While it can be a more profitable line of work, sales may also require some travel, so make sure to look into this possibility while applying.

For more information on sales jobs,
see pages 33 through 39.

Please note: As of this publication, all links should lead directly to the job site. The author is not responsible for moved or broken links that may occur after publication. All job descriptions come directly from the company's job listing(s).

Sales Jobs

1. <u>A Better Call: Business Development Representative:</u> If you excel at appointment setting or cold calling, we need to talk. Our best Business Development Representatives earn in excess of $20.00/hour. A Better Call, Inc. is a successful, respected, business to business telemarketing company located in Canton, MA. Since 1995, we have helped businesses achieve their sales goals through appointment setting. We are looking for the best of the best; enthusiastic, motivated, part time with potential for full time, lead generation representatives. This work from home position is 100% phone work. Our ideal candidate will have the ability to think on their feet and have a proven track record of successful cold calling to generate qualified face-to-face meetings. This candidate will have a strong business background with experience presenting to C-Level executives. You must be highly motivated, reliable, and a disciplined self-starter. You take ownership of a project and are persistent and effective when faced with a challenge. Basic computer and typing skills are required. Experience with ACT contact software is a plus.

    https://abettercall.com/telemarketing_employment_opportunities.html

2. <u>A Place for Mom: Senior Living Advisor:</u> Senior Living Advisors (SLAs) are inside sales representatives responsible for educating families on senior care options and referring them to customer communities that match their needs. The Senior Living Advisor refers pre-screened internet leads and follows up with the family throughout

the search process. Senior Living Advisors are also responsible for coordinating with customers to ensure timely follow-up to referred families. Our SLAs act as the liaison between families in need and the senior housing communities or care providers.

https://careers-aplaceformom.icims.com/jobs/

3. Aliera Companies: Inside Sales Agent: We are seeking individuals to join a dynamic, high energy Inside Sales team! As a full-time Inside Sales Health Insurance Agent, you are responsible for selling HealthCare plans and benefits to pre-qualified contacts.

https://productinfo.alieracompanies.com/about/careers/opportunities/

4. Aon: Various: Aon virtual jobs include Senior Associate, Support Analyst, and more.

http://jobs.aon.com/

5. BroadPath Healthcare Solutions: Health Insurance Agent - Sales: BroadPath Healthcare Solutions is actively hiring remote, work from home, Licensed Health Insurance Sales Agents. Our most successful agents are collaborative, disciplined, sincere, and bring accountability to their work. Licensed Health Insurance Sales Agents are responsible for responding to inbound calls from individuals interested in purchasing health plans and making outbound calls to individuals who have requested additional information or follow-up. As a work-from-home associate, BroadPath will provide you with a laptop, 4 port USB hub, Bhive web camera, and USB headset.

http://www.broad-path.com/join-our-team/careers/

6. Cruise.com: Cruise Sales Agents: Requires at least two years of recent cruise sales work experience, preferably in a call center environment, selling all of the major cruise lines. Language fluency in

both English and Spanish is required for some openings. Our cyber sales agents sell cruise vacations and other leisure travel options to potential customers through inbound telephone calls, outbound calls, and email leads. Our cyber sales agents are expert closers and are adept at upselling cruise vacations to maximize the customer experience as well as revenue. We are seeking true sales professionals who can meet or exceed minimum monthly sales productivity goals to maximize their financial reward. These positions offer base pay plus a tiered incentive plan.

https://www.cruise.com/cruise-information/employment/

7. DVMelite: Telecommuting Sales Representative: You will work 30 hours weekly, Monday-Friday during business hours for a 100% remote company. You will be responsible for your computer and high speed internet and will be working warm leads from various marketing sources. Hourly pay plus commissions will be paid, making this an excellent work from home position for the ambitious sales professional.

https://dvmelite.recruitpro.com/jobs/89074.html

8. Extended Presence: Sr. Qualified Appointment Setting Veteran: Ideal candidates will have experience prospecting C-Level, VP Level and/or Director Level contacts at mid-tier companies, large companies, and Fortune 500 companies. This requires the ability to deliver a strong eloquent value proposition, understand and qualify a client's needs, assess business issues/pain points, and set qualified sales appointments.

http://extendedpresence.com/current-opportunities.html

9. First Data: Sales Executive: Responsible for new account selling to regional merchant chains or community banks with moderate

length sales cycles. These are individual salespeople below the national account or strategic account level, but above the transactional or short cycle account level. Medium to long sales cycle. Works independently under broad supervision and general instruction (Solution Specialist).

> https://fdc.taleo.net/careersection/fdc_external/jobsearch

10. <u>Hibu: Digital Account Executive:</u> As a Digital Account Executive you will partner with small to medium sized business clients to create effective Digital Marketing programs that bring increased revenues to their business. You will be accountable for achieving and exceeding sales objectives which are a result of selling our diversified digital programs.

> https://recruiting2.ultipro.com/HIB1000HIBU/JobBoard/f4d92cb8-5c63-4d45-89e2-d1d6c6c154b9/?q=&o=postedDateDesc

11. <u>Intelliverse: Remote Business Development Representative:</u> Intelliverse is seeking an energetic and outgoing Lead Generation Specialist with a minimum of two years of lead generation/inside sales experience. The Lead Generation Specialist is responsible for prospecting, qualifying, and generating sales leads. This individual will be a highly motivated self-starter and able to identify and develop new business prospects from multiple sources including inbound marketing leads, prospect lists, discovery, and individual research. A dynamic personality with a drive to reach decision makers is essential.

> https://www.intelliverse.com/company/careers.shtml

12. <u>Philips: Various:</u> You know you're a valuable asset and so do we. As a vital member of our Philips' Sales team, you will be right at the heart of our business. Our Sales function is fundamental to driving

growth and profitability. As an active contributor, you will want to have your finger on the pulse of what next-generation users want when it comes to new experiences, products, and services, constantly learning and collaborating to make these insights a reality.

https://www.careers.philips.com/professional/global/en/c/sales-jobs

13. RiseSmart: Resume Writer: RiseSmart is a leading provider of outplacement and career management services. We are seeking experienced resume writers to join our team. RiseSmart's innovative approach to human capital management has earned the company a wide range of awards and recognition from organizations including Bersin by Deloitte, the Best in Biz, Gartner Inc., the Golden Bridge Awards, Red Herring, the Stevie Awards, and TIE.

 https://www.randstadrisesmart.com/careers-open-positions

14. SalesFish: Virtual Sales Agent: We are ALWAYS looking for great Virtual Sales Agents to "stock" our talent pool. If the criteria listed on our site fits or almost fits what you are looking for, throw us a "line" telling us your fish stories and why you think you could thrive in our environment.

 https://www.salesfish.com/job_opportunities.cfm

15. SalesRoads: Appointment Setting, Lead Generation & Sales Professionals: Our appointment setting, lead generation, and sales positions are work from home employment opportunities where you can schedule flexible hours and work out of your home office. SalesRoads Sales Development Reps work with clients to call into business executives from a list provided and schedule qualified appointments, generate leads, or sell products and services.

 https://salesroads.com/careers/#.UYZ1-qJO-9k

16. <u>Sanofi: Various:</u> As a company that respects cultural differences, Sanofi depends on the diversity and talents of its employees to be more innovative, effective, and competitive.

    https://jobs.sanofi.us/search-jobs/remote

17. <u>Travel Leaders Group: Travel Sales Specialist:</u> As a Sales Specialist, you will be the "right and left hand" to two (2) Senior Travel Agents, providing them and their clients with a broad range of support and services related to the lifecycle of each booking. Your contribution and attention to detail are vital to the agent's sales success and clients' satisfaction.

    https://careers-travelleaders.icims.com/jobs/search?

18. <u>TTEC: Various:</u> Looking for a reliable, fulfilling, flexible job that you can do from the comfort of your own home? TTEC@Home could be the perfect solution!

    https://www.ttecjobs.com/en/careers?

19. <u>WL Marketing: Account Manager/Customer Service Representative:</u> As an account manager, you will be responsible for maintaining the relationship with our clients, making sure that their work is done precisely according to their specifications, exploring their needs, and creatively coming up with solutions/helping develop products (from the pieces we have) that will address their problems, as well as documenting processes that come up. Many of our clients can be large and short on time, so availability throughout the day (with instant phone pickup) is a necessity. You will also be given interested clients/good fits and be responsible for opening new accounts, including cold calling, reaching out via social media, and following

up to close the deal. Your time would be spent around 50-90% on existing accounts and 10-50% on opening new ones.

https://www.wlmarketing.com/jobs.html

TRANSCRIPTION INTRO

Do you have a keen eye (and ear) for detail?

Were you the fastest typer in your high school computer class? *raises hand*

Are you somewhat of a master at listening to and dissecting other people's conversations?

If you answered yes to any (or all) of these questions, check out the transcription jobs on pages 43 through 47.

What does it take to be a transcriptionist? Like other categories, it begins with a high-speed internet connection but also takes a great word processor and lightning-fast typing skills. When you work as a transcriptionist, you can plan to cover everything from typing work dictations to writing memoirs or transcribing legal documents.

Please note: As of this publication, all links should lead directly to the job site. The author is not responsible for moved or broken links that may occur after publication. All job descriptions come directly from the company's job listing(s).

Transcription Jobs

1. <u>3Play Media:</u> Contract position to transcribe recorded English audio and edit imperfect transcription using our proprietary internet-based software.

    https://www.3playmedia.com/company/jobs/contract-work/

2. <u>AccuTran Global:</u> We are always interested in engaging with new contract transcribers, real-time stenographers, and voice writers. We offer work in other departments to contractors who have an established track record with us. The ability to work independently and meet client deadlines while following guidelines precisely is critical for anyone contracting with us.

    http://www.accutranglobal.com/

3. <u>Allegis:</u> Allegis specializes in transcription for the insurance and legal industries. Our work-from-home transcriptionists transcribe recorded audio files for some of the largest providers in the country. This means a sizable and steady workflow that satisfies transcription contracts of many types and sizes.

    https://www.allegistranscription.com/transcription-services/transcription-jobs/

4. <u>Babbletype:</u> The transcripts we produce are mission-critical parts of market research projects. Completeness, accuracy, and reliability are absolute requirements.

    http://babbletype.com/apply-for-work

5. <u>Birch Creek Communications:</u> We have openings in our transcription department for high quality corporate transcriptionists, transcribing audio files for our corporate clients. We do not do any medical or legal transcription.

    http://www.birchcreekcommunications.com/3894/index.html

6. <u>Captionmax:</u> At Captionmax, you can be a part of a dedicated team working to make media accessible to a wide and inclusive audience.

    https://www.captionmax.com/workwithus/

7. <u>CastingWords:</u> Freelancers: Transcribe, edit, and complete other short jobs online, at your own pace. Work as much or as little as you want, when you want. No fees - we pay you, you don't pay us.

    https://workshop.castingwords.com/

8. <u>Daily Transcription:</u> We're excited that you're interested in one of our openings! Daily Transcription provides services to entertainment, corporate, and legal industries as well as to academic institutions.

    - https://www.dailytranscription.com/career-english/

9. <u>GMR Transcription:</u> We value our team of transcriptionists and pride ourselves in the wonderful relationships we have built with them. We strive to provide valuable feedback to transcriptionists, so they can continue to grow in terms of knowledge, experience, and

proficiency. As a result, we have highly satisfied transcriptionists who enjoy working with us and a low staff turnover rate.

> https://www.gmrtranscription.com/careers.aspx

10. <u>GoTranscript:</u> GoTranscript is a thriving web-based transcription and translation company. We're always looking to fill our open freelance transcription jobs so we can grow our team and keep pace with customer orders. If you're a skilled transcriptionist who takes pride in your work, and you want to make a difference in the world, we want you!

    > https://gotranscript.com/transcription-jobs

11. <u>Net Transcripts:</u> If you value innovation, hard work, and fun as much as we do, we invite you to join our team!

    > https://www.nettranscripts.com/careers.htm

12. <u>QuickTate:</u> Quicktate transcribes voicemail messages, memos, letters, legal files, medical files, recordings of phone calls, conference calls, and other audio files.

    > https://typists.quicktate.com/transcribers/signup

13. <u>Rev:</u> Want to enjoy the flexibility of working from anywhere? Work from home as a transcriptionist with Rev. To get started, you'll need strong English skills, a computer, and a dependable Internet connection.

    > https://www.rev.com/freelancers/transcription

14. <u>Scribie:</u> Transcribe audio files into text.

    > https://scribie.com/jobs

15. SpeakWrite: We are accepting applications for qualified typing and transcription experts to join our team and get paid to help facilitate the work of professionals all over the country!

    https://speakwrite.com/transcription-jobs/

16. Speechpad: As a transcriber, you'll listen to audio files or watch videos and type out whatever is spoken. Whether you're a seasoned transcriber or a novice, you can probably find transcription jobs that are appropriate for your experience level. If you are new to Speechpad, this is where you should start.

    https://www.speechpad.com/worker/jobs

17. SyncScript: We are looking for transcriptionists to work remotely from the US. Transcribers have the flexibility to set their own schedules, working as much as they'd like. We ask that you are available for a minimum of 3 sound hours per week.

    https://syncscripts.com/apply-here/

18. Tigerfish: Tigerfish has been in business since 1989. We are known to our clients for delivering work that is on time, impeccably written, error-free, and thoroughly researched. For this we depend upon an elite team of transcribers. If you feel you have the skills to produce work that is up to our standards, we invite you to apply.

    https://tigerfish.com/applicants/

19. TranscribeMe: We offer the opportunity to be a part of our unique community at one of the best transcription companies and create lasting connections with professionals all over the world. All you need is a computer, a reliable Internet connection, and the ability to transcribe audio and video in any of the languages that we support.

    https://www.transcribeme.com/transcription-jobs

20. TransPerfect: The world's top companies trust TransPerfect to help them excel in the global marketplace.

    https://transperfect.wd5.myworkdayjobs.com/transperfect

21. Ubiqus: Ubiqus is continuously searching for qualified, talented individuals to join our team of language, transcription, and event professionals.

    https://www.ubiqus.com/contact-us/jobs/

22. Verbal Ink: We're always looking for highly skilled linguists to add to our growing team.

    https://www.verbalink.io/company/contact/jobs/

WRITING INTRO

Writing from home has a place near and dear to my heart. Why? Well, it is what I do for a living and is what gave me my start in the work-from-home realm! Fortunately, companies are always looking for high-quality writers, so if you have a knack for the English language, you may be able to make a great living from the jobs listed on the following pages.

In addition to writing jobs, the following pages contain editing positions as well as curriculum creators and content development.

Please note: As of this publication, all links should lead directly to the job site. The author is not responsible for moved or broken links that may occur after publication. All job descriptions come directly from the company's job listing(s).

Writing Jobs

1. Cactus Global: Editing (Various): Telecommute jobs are just as important as office-based ones. At CACTUS, you can join a team of highly skilled writers and editors who are experts in various academic fields. Our constant efforts to be a freelancer-friendly organization have resulted in us being ranked among the Top 20 Companies with Remote Jobs for 3 years running.

   https://www.cactusglobal.com/careers/work-from-home#wfh

2. Coalition Technologies: Copywriter: We are a fast-growing SEO and Web Design firm located in Culver City. We are looking to hire freelance copywriters and copy editors to edit original content for our client's websites.CT offers the opportunity to work with a highly collaborative, industry-leading team. Quality of service is always our #1 priority. As a result, our innovative digital marketing professionals work relentlessly to provide outstanding quality services for our clients.

   https://app.testedrecruits.com/posting/5230

3. Course Hero: Item Writer: Course Hero is scaling! Are you looking to leverage your subject matter expertise to help students learn? Course Hero is looking for item writers who will author high-quality solutions to questions.. Our ideal candidate will have a strong expertise ranging from general biology, human anatomy and physiology to organismal biology. Candidates must be self-starters with

a passion for teaching, an outstanding work ethic, and a positive attitude.

https://www.coursehero.com/jobs/#positions

4. <u>DistanceWeb: Various:</u> DistanceWeb is currently searching for freelancers in a number of areas. Web Design. Web Development. Copywriters. Project Managers. If you are a talented web junkie in any of these areas, we want to hear from you. Please contact us at jobs@distanceweb.net for more information. Include a text copy of your resume as well as URLs to any relevant bodies of work online.

http://distanceweb.net/about_join.shtml

5. <u>Eagle Productivity Solutions: Curriculum / Content Writers:</u> The team at Eagle works to design and deliver industry-leading training content, from live, instructor-led training to video to dynamic reference pieces. Our Writers are responsible for successfully executing curriculum development projects.

https://eagleproductivity.com/careers.html

6. <u>Get A Copywriter: Copywriter:</u> We make it fast and easy to get great content written by experts who truly comprehend what you want to say before they even start writing. Our thoughtful assignment process carefully matches your job with an appropriately skilled writer, and ensures your satisfaction by seeing that all your requirements are plainly communicated in advance.

https://secure.getacopywriter.com/copywriter-signup

7. <u>HiringThing: Various:</u> HiringThing is a fully remote, cloud-based software company that helps companies post jobs online, manage applicants, and hire great employees. We believe that everyone should be free to craft his or her own perfect work environment.

We care about results produced, flexibility, and results, not butts in chairs. If you would like to be part of a company that values your ideas and contributions, we encourage you to apply for one of the open positions.

https://careers.hiringthing.com/

8. **HVMN: Various:** H.V.M.N. is Health Via Modern Nutrition. A healthier, smarter society is a better society. Let's build and live in that future together.

https://jobs.lever.co/hvmn

9. **International Association of Professional Writers & Educators: Writers & Editors:** This position will involve writing and/or editing articles and blog posts on a wide range of topics.

https://iapwe.org/apply-49553/

10. **iWriter: Writer:** iWriter is the fastest, easiest and most reliable way to have content written for your website. You'll be able to post a project and 1000s of freelance writers from across the globe will have instant access to write your content quickly, professionally, and affordably.

https://www.iwriter.com/writer-application

11. **METRO: Content Development:** METRO is the "go-to" provider of content and data services for many of your favorite brands and online retailers around the globe. As a community member, you have access to an ever-growing list of projects to work on. METRO makes it easy for you to work from anywhere and at any time. So whether you're an early bird or a night owl, you're always a click away from your next project.

https://metro.cnetcontent.com/

12. <u>Narcity Media: Freelance Writer:</u> Narcity writers are ambitious and independent thinkers who know what millennials care about. Our writers want to be the best source of information for their communities, whether it's breaking down new legislation, spotlighting extraordinary local characters, or finding new festivals that everyone should know about.

    https://www.narcitymedia.com/jobs/

13. <u>NextWave Advocacy: Grassroots Writer:</u> Writers for NextWave's campaigns help constituents share their stories with government officials and the public. Advocates may communicate their opinions in letters to policymakers, in comments to regulatory agencies, in op-eds submitted to local newspapers, or in content posted online.

    http://www.nextwaveathome.com/write/

14. <u>RiseSmart: Resume Writer:</u> RiseSmart is a leading provider of outplacement and career management services. We are seeking experienced resumé writers to join our team. RiseSmart's innovative approach to human capital management has earned the company a wide range of awards and recognition from organizations including Bersin by Deloitte, the Best in Biz, Gartner Inc., the Golden Bridge Awards, Red Herring, the Stevie Awards, and TIE.

    https://www.risesmart.com/about-risesmart/careers/careers-open-positions

15. <u>Scribe Media: Freelance:</u> Writing, publishing, and marketing books is what we do, but helping people tell their story and share their knowledge to leave a legacy of impact—that is who we are.

    https://scribemedia.com/join/

16. <u>SmartBrief: Freelance:</u> SmartBrief brings you the most important business news. Our editors curate top stories from more than 10000 credible sources & summarize them for you.

    https://jobs.silkroad.com/SmartBrief/

17. <u>Speechpad: Various:</u> Speechpad offers a variety of jobs to suit your skills, aptitude, and experience. New workers generally start out as transcribers doing general transcription. As an entry level transcriber, you'll find there are plenty of advancement opportunities to move into roles that afford higher pay and greater responsibility. For example, after becoming an experienced transcriber with a high rating, you could advance to the reviewer role, where you would be editing the work of other transcribers. Or, you could also become a captioner. In that role, you'll start off doing video transcription and eventually learn to work with our captioning console as a captioning reviewer. If you are an experienced translator, we have work for you as well.

    https://www.speechpad.com/worker/jobs

18. <u>Talent, Inc.: Resume Writer:</u> Using our proprietary technology, you will work hand in hand with job seekers to craft their new resumés, cover letters, and Linkedin profiles. Our technology is designed specifically with writers in mind. We provide all of the tools and support you need to be a successful writer!

    https://www.talentinc.com/job?id=224

19. <u>Textbroker: Author:</u> Is writing your passion? Then Textbroker is the right place for you. Since 2005, Textbroker is the leading provider of unique, custom content. Thousands of registered authors and customers from around the globe execute more than 100,000 content orders through Textbroker every month. Our clients, including

publicly traded corporations, small business owners, e-commerce websites, social media communities, and publishing houses require a broad variety of content.

https://www.textbroker.com/authors

20. <u>Verblio: Freelance:</u> Grow your writing career with the simplest, most flexible freelance gig out there.

https://www.verblio.com/become-a-writer

21. <u>WL Marketing: Article Writer:</u> This is a part time position to help create alternative news content much like disinfo.com, politicallore.com, and politicalblindspot.com.

https://www.wlmarketing.com/articlewriter.html

Why I Advise Against MLMs

What do religion, politics, sex, and MLM all have in common?

You should never talk about them at parties or family reunions.

I know, I know: this sounds super harsh, but here is the cold, hard truth to it--most MLMs will make you lose money. I am not making this up and here is the proof: According to the Consumer Awareness Institute[1], more than 73% of people who join an MLM will either lose money or make no money at all, with some companies and uplines even encouraging members to go into debt with the promise of making it back, plus some (source[2]). As if all of this was not unsettling enough, the Federal Trade Commission[3] (yes, THE government agency that was put into place to protect consumers) has also reported a 99.6% loss rate on these well-known direct sales companies:

Advocare
Ameriplan
Amway
Arbonne
CyberwizeFortune
Hi-Tech Marketing
FreeLife International
Herbalife

Immunotec
iNetGlobal
Isagenix
Mannatech
Melaleuca
Mona Vie
MXI Corp.
Nikken

Nu Skin	USANA
Relive	Vollara
SendOutCards	World Ventures
Sunrider	XANGO
Symmetry	Yor Health
Tahitian Noni International	Your Travel Biz
Tupperware	

If it were only a matter of signing up to be a distributor and maybe paying a one-time fee (of less than $100), I would not be so suspicious of MLMs; however, these models encourage you not only to sell, but recruit (which is typically how you make most of your money--via your downline), plus meet a monthly quota in order not to lose your rank, company-bought car, bonus, etc. Too often, when someone isn't meeting their quota or wants to jump to the next rank, they will buy products themselves, making what could already be a bad situation even worse.

While I have personally never been part of an MLM, I have several friends who have (spoiler: none of them stuck with it because they were either losing money, not recruiting or making sales, or realized that the model - not their hard work - is flawed), as well as parents who were in a popular catalog-based MLM for 10+ years and did everything by the book, only to come out in the negative. While most direct sales companies (and uplines) claim there is money to be made if you put in the time and effort, this simply is not the case, which is demonstrated in this article by the HuffPost[4] that tells the heartbreaking stories of Angela and Sandra, who put in 60+ hours a week and have nothing to show for it.

Look: If you are part of the 1% who has made it in your MLM, I sincerely congratulate you; you have conquered the odds and have

THE BEST WORK-FROM-HOME JOBS FOR 2020

obviously built a successful direct sales business. If you are just starting out, however, and have no money to spare for sign-up fees, products, website, monthly quota, etc., I STRONGLY encourage you to look into the aforementioned jobs in this book. One of the biggest pro-MLM arguments that I hear is that you have to pay for no-skid shoes, gas, black slacks, etc. to work at McDonald's, so why not invest that same amount into your "own" business that you can do from the comfort of your own home? Well, the answer is relatively simple: You are guaranteed to be making a certain amount at McDonald's, as you are an hourly (or maybe even salary, if you work in management) employee, whereas you can make nothing (or even lose money) via an MLM, where you are not necessarily paid for your hours worked.

For more information on MLMs and the risks associated with starting a direct sales business, please check out the following resources:

Sounds Like MLM But Ok Podcast
Reddit Anti-MLM
Sounds Like MLM But Ok Facebook
Roberta Blevins
The Dream Podcast
Multilevel Marketing: Last Night Tonight with John Oliver

About Annie

Annie Sandmeier is a wife, stay-at-home-mom, black coffee enthusiast, Cradle Catholic, and writer whose work is read by thousands every day.

With an education and background in Broadcast Journalism, Annie's plan was always to take over Adele Arakawa's seat at 9News Denver (after Arakawa retired, of course!), but marrying out of college and having her first son shortly thereafter changed her focus, leading Annie to look more into work-from-home opportunities. After working remotely as her hometown museum's marketing coordinator, Annie began writing for a popular website, which is when she realized she was making more money writing (very) part-time than she did as a full-time reporter. Since this realization, Annie has been working hard to help other moms find legitimate work-from-home work, leading to the creation of Side Hustle Mom (and, 2 years later, this book).

When Annie isn't writing or hustling like a mother, you can find her going on adventures with her 2 boys, planning the next big vacation with her husband, hosting or attending play dates, volunteering at her oldest's school, or drinking wine and/or coffee with friends (don't judge).

About Side Hustle Mom

Side Hustle Mom was founded in 2017 as a way to help other stay-at-home moms find legitimate, remote work that allows them to make money from home whilst raising their babies. Since its founding, Side Hustle Mom has grown to become a popular resource for not only moms, but also dads, students, retirees, or those just looking to escape that 9 to 5 cubicle grind. Whether you try your hand at FBA, selling designer duds on eBay, writing and/or editing on a freelance basis, or creating beautiful jewelry to sell at a local boutique, we want to be here to help and support you every step of the way!

For more information on Side Hustle Mom, or to access our free work-from-home job board or This Week in Job listings, please visit our website.

References

1 Taylor, John M. "Chapter 8: MLM – A LITANY OF MISREPRESENTATIONS." *The Case (for and) against Multi-Level Marketing*, Federal Trade Commission, 2011, https://www.ftc.gov/sites/default/files/documents/public_comments/trade-regulation-rule-disclosure-requirements-and-prohibitions-concerning-business-opportunities-ftc.r511993-00010 /00010-57283.pdf.

2 Wicker, Alden. "Multilevel-Marketing Companies like LuLaRoe Are Forcing People into Debt and Psychological Crisis." *Quartz*, 6 Aug. 2017, https://qz.com/1039331/mlms-like-avon-and-lularoe-are-sending-people-into-debt-and-psychological-crisis/?utm_source=pocket&utm_medium=email&utm_campaign=pockethits&fbclid=IwAR3ttgIURd5sn0cMT6T31yQYE8e-AHm4R-i1wWxbPIPTJjtvoMKMQjeFi1D8.

3 Taylor, John M. "Chapter 8: MLM – A LITANY OF MISREPRESENTATIONS." *The Case (for and) against Multi-Level Marketing*, Federal Trade Commission, 2011, https://www.ftc.gov/sites/default/files/documents/public_comments/trade-regulation-rule-disclosure-requirements-and-prohibitions-concerning-business-opportunities-ftc.r511993-00010 /00010-57283.pdf.

4 **4.** Bond, Casey. "MLMs Are A Nightmare For Women And Everyone They Know." *Huffington Post*, Verizon Media, 27 June 2019, https://www.huffpost.com/entry/mlm-pyramid-scheme-target-women-financial-freedom_l_5d0bfd60e4b07ae90d9a6a9e?guccounter=1&guce_referrer=aHR0cHM6Ly93d3cuZ29vZ2xlLmNvbS8&guce_referrer_sig=AQAAAI-o7RPDmdzeOtWsI1kD6VobFJpbbdqa46NAwmmG7KU6QMro6mzQZ1I5ZjkUTmKq9MClUuqlFl4mJr7B1PA6pIb67Lm5G3yqmUnSEgRjf7smaL_HMF1BPW10xmkibBomg0t8-MZzF5vA-2h4rv8yDiVmeve0Y4JPjFGqK4VpdvU.

Made in the USA
Monee, IL
16 March 2020